LOVE'S ENCHANTMENT

LOVE'S ENCHANTMENT

STORY POEMS

AND BALLADS

COLLECTED BY

HELEN FERRIS

DECORATED BY

VERA BOCK

Granger Index Reprint Series

BOOKS FOR LIBRARIES PRESS

FREEPORT, NEW YORK

STANDARD BOOK NUMBER:

8369-6076-9

LIBRARY OF CONGRESS CATALOG CARD NUMBER:

73-86796

MANUFACTURED
BY
HALLMARK LITHOGRAPHERS, INC.
IN THE U.S.A.

CONTENTS

To

my dear

JENNIE MEAD

who is brave

and gallant

and gay

LADY CLARE

I T WAS THE TIME when lilies blow,
  And clouds are highest up in air,
Lord Ronald brought a lily-white doe
  To give his cousin, Lady Clare.

I trow they did not part in scorn—
  Lovers long-betrothed were they;
They two will wed the morrow morn;
  God's blessing on the day!

"He does not love me for my birth,
  Nor for my lands so broad and fair;
He loves me for my own true worth,
  And that is well," said Lady Clare.

In there came old Alice the nurse,
  Said, "Who was this that went from thee?"
"It was my cousin," said Lady Clare,
  "Tomorrow he weds with me."

"O God be thanked!" said Alice the nurse,
  "That all comes round so just and fair;
Lord Ronald is heir of all your lands,
  And you are not the Lady Clare."

"Are ye out of your mind, my nurse, my nurse,"
  Said Lady Clare, "that ye speak so wild?"
"As God's above," said Alice the nurse,
  "I speak the truth, you are my child.

"The old Earl's daughter died at my breast;
  I speak the truth as I live by bread!
I buried her like my own sweet child,
  And put my child in her stead."

"Falsely, falsely have ye done,
  O, mother," she said, "if this be true,
To keep the best man under the sun
  So many years from his due."

"Nay now, my child," said Alice the nurse,
  "But keep the secret for your life,
And all you have will be Lord Ronald's,
  When you are man and wife."

"If I'm a beggar born," she said,
  "I will speak out, for I dare not lie.
Pull off, pull off the brooch of gold,
  And fling the diamond necklace by."

"Nay now, my child," said Alice the nurse,
    "But keep the secret all ye can."
She said: "Not so, but I will know
    If there be faith in man."

"Nay now, what faith?" said Alice the nurse;
    "The man will cleave unto his right."
"And he shall have it," the lady replied,
    "Though I should die tonight."

"Yet give one kiss to your mother dear!
    Alas, my child, I sinned for thee."
"O mother, mother, mother," she said,
    "So strange it seems to me.

"Yet here's a kiss for my mother dear,
    My mother dear, if this be so,
And lay your hand upon my head,
    And bless me, mother, ere I go."

She clad herself in a russet gown,
    She was no longer Lady Clare;
She went by dale, she went by down,
    With a single rose in her hair.

The lily-white doe Lord Ronald had brought
    Leapt up from where she lay,
Dropt her head in the maiden's hand,
    And followed her all the way.

Down stept Lord Ronald from his tower:
    "O Lady Clare, you shame your worth!
Why come you drest like a village maid,
    That are the flower of the earth?"

"If I come drest like a village maid,
    I am but as my fortunes are;
I am a beggar born," she said,
    "And not the Lady Clare."

"Play me no tricks," said Lord Ronald,
    "For I am yours in word and deed."
"Play me no tricks," said Lord Ronald,
    "Your riddle is hard to read."

O and proudly stood she up!
    Her heart within her did not fail;
She looked into Lord Ronald's eyes,
    And told him all her nurse's tale.

He laughed a laugh of merry scorn;
    He turned and kissed her where she stood.
"If you are not the heiress born,
    And I," said he, "the next in blood—

"If you are not the heiress born,
    And I," said he, "the lawful heir,
We two will wed tomorrow morn,
    And you will still be Lady Clare."

Alfred Tennyson

ROBIN HOOD AND ALLEN-A-DALE

COME, LISTEN TO ME, you gallants so free,
   All you that love mirth for to hear,
And I will tell you of a bold outlaw,
   That lived in Nottinghamshire.

As Robin Hood in the forest stood,
   All under the greenwood tree,
There was he ware of a brave young man,
   As fine as fine might be.

The youngster was clothed in scarlet red,
   In scarlet fine and gay,
And he did frisk it over the plain,
   And chanted a roundelay.

As Robin Hood next morning stood,
   Amongst the leaves so gay,
There did he spy the same young man
   Come drooping along the way.

The scarlet he wore the day before,
    It was clean cast away;
And every step he fetched a sigh,
    "Alack! and well-a-day!"

Then stepped forth brave Little John,
    And Nick, the miller's son,
Which made the young man bend his bow,
    When as he saw them come.

"Stand off! stand off!" the young man said;
    "What is your will with me?"
"You must come before our master straight
    Under yon greenwood tree."

And when he came bold Robin before,
    Robin asked him courteously,
"O, hast thou any money to spare
    For my merry men and me?"

"I have no money," the young man said,
    "But five shillings and a ring;
And that I have kept this seven long years,
    To have it at my wedding.

"Yesterday I should have married a maid,
    But she is now from me ta'en,
And chosen to be an old knight's delight,
    Whereby my poor heart is slain."

"What is thy name?" then said Robin Hood;
    "Come tell me without any fail."
"By the faith of my body," then said the young man,
    "My name it is Allen-a-Dale."

"What wilt thou give me," said Robin Hood,
    "In ready gold or fee,
To help thee to thy truelove again,
    And deliver her unto thee?"

"I have no money," then quoth the young man,
    "No ready gold nor fee,
But I will swear upon a book
    Thy true servant for to be."

"How many miles is it to thy truelove?
    Come tell me without any guile."
"By the faith of my body," then said the young man,
    "It is but five little mile."

Then Robin he hasted over the plain,
    He did neither stint nor lin,
Until he came unto the church
    Where Allen should keep his wedding.

"What dost thou here?" the bishop he said,
    "I prithee now tell to me."
"I am a bold harper," quoth Robin Hood,
    "And the best in the north country."

"O, welcome, O, welcome," the bishop he said,
    "That music best pleaseth me."
"You shall have no music," quoth Robin Hood,
    "Till the bride and bridegroom I see."

With that came in a wealthy knight,
    Which was both grave and old,
And after him a finikin lass,
    Did shine like glistering gold.

"This is no fit match," quoth bold Robin Hood,
    "That you do seem to make here;
But since we are come unto the church,
    The bride she shall choose her own dear."

Then Robin Hood put his horn to his mouth,
    And blew blasts two or three;
When four and twenty bowmen bold
    Came leaping over the lea.

And when they came into the churchyard,
    Marching all in a row,
The first man was Allen-a-Dale,
    To give bold Robin his bow.

"This is thy truelove," Robin he said,
    "Young Allen, as I hear say;
And you shall be married at this same time,
    Before we depart away."

8

"That shall not be," the bishop he said,
  "For thy word shall not stand;
They shall be three times asked in the church,
  As the law is of our land."

Robin Hood pulled off the bishop's coat,
  And put it upon Little John;
"By the faith of my body," then Robin said,
  "This cloth doth make thee a man."

When Little John went into the choir,
  The people began for to laugh;
He asked them seven times in the church,
  Lest three times should not be enough.

"Who gives me this maid?" then said Little John;
  Quoth Robin, "That do I,
And he that doth take her from Allen-a-Dale
  Full dearly he shall her buy."

And thus having ended this merry wedding,
  The bride looked as fresh as a queen,
And so they returned to the merry green Wood,
  Amongst the leaves so green.

An Old Ballad

THE FORSAKEN MERMAN

Come, dear children, let us away;
Down and away below!
Now my brothers call from the bay,
Now the great winds shoreward blow,
Now the salt tides seaward flow;
Now the wild white horses play,
Champ and chafe and toss in the spray.
Children dear, let us away!
This way, this way!

Call her once before you go—
Call once yet!
In a voice that she will know:
"Margaret! Margaret!"
Children's voices should be dear
(Call once more) to a mother's ear
Children's voices, wild with pain—
Surely she will come again!
Call her once and come away;

This way, this way!
"Mother dear, we cannot stay!
The wild white horses foam and fret."
Margaret! Margaret!

Come, dear children, come away down;
Call no more!
One last look at the white-walled town,
And the little gray church on the windy shore;
Then come down!
She will not come though you call all day;
Come away, come away!

Children dear, was it yesterday
We heard the sweet bells over the bay?
In the caverns where we lay,
Through the surf and through the swell,
The far-off sound of a silver bell?
Sand-strewn caverns, cool and deep,
Where the winds are all asleep;
Where the spent lights quiver and gleam,
Where the salt weed sways in the stream,
Where the sea-beasts, ranged all round,
Feed in the ooze of their pasture ground;
Where the sea-snakes coil and twine,
Dry their mail and bask in the brine;
Where great whales come sailing by,
Sail and sail, with unshut eye,

Round the world for ever and aye?
When did music come this way?
Children dear, was it yesterday?

Children dear, was it yesterday
(Call yet once) that she went away?
Once she sate with you and me,
On a red-gold throne in the heart of the sea,
And the youngest sate on her knee.
She combed its bright hair, and she tended it well,
When down swung the sound of a far-off bell.
She sighed, she looked up through the clear green sea;
She said: "I must go, for my kinsfolk pray
In the little gray church on the shore today.
'Twill be Easter-time in the world—ah me!
And I lose my poor soul, Merman! here with thee."
I said: "Go up, dear heart, through the waves;
Say thy prayer, and come back to the kind sea-caves!"
She smiled, she went up through the surf in the bay.
Children dear, was it yesterday?

Children dear, were we long alone?
"The sea grows stormy, the little ones moan;
Long prayers," I said, "in the world they say;
Come!" I said; and we rose through the surf in the bay.
We went up the beach, by the sandy down
Where the sea-stocks bloom, to the white-walled town;
Through the narrow-paved streets, where all was still,

To the little gray church on the windy hill.
From the church came a murmur of folk at their prayers,
But we stood without in the cold blowing airs.

We climbed on the graves, on the stones worn with rains,
And we gazed up the aisle through the small leaded panes.
She sate by the pillar; we saw her clear:
"Margaret, hist! come quick, we are here!
Dear heart," I said, "we are long alone;
The sea grows stormy, the little ones moan."
But, ah, she gave me never a look,
For her eyes were sealed to the holy book!
Loud prays the priest; shut stands the door.
Come away, children, call no more!
Come away, come down, call no more!

Down, down, down!
Down to the depths of the sea!
She sits at her wheel in the humming town,
Singing most joyfully.
Hark what she sings: "O joy, O joy,
For the humming street, and the child with its toy!
For the priest, and the bell, and the holy well;
For the wheel where I spun,
And the blessed light of the sun!"
And so she sings her fill,
Singing most joyfully,
Till the spindle drops from her hand,

And the whizzing wheel stands still.
She steals to the window, and looks at the sand,
And over the sand at the sea;
And her eyes are set in a stare;
And anon there breaks a sigh,
And anon there drops a tear,
From a sorrow-clouded eye,
And a heart sorrow-laden,
A long, long sigh,
For the cold strange eyes of a little Mermaiden
And the gleam of her golden hair.

Come away, away, children;
Come, children, come down!
The hoarse wind blows coldly;
Lights shine in the town.
She will start from her slumber
When gusts shake the door;
She will hear the winds howling,
Will hear the waves roar.
We shall see, while above us
The waves roar and whirl,
A ceiling of amber,
A pavement of pearl,
Singing: "Here came a mortal,
But faithless was she!
And alone dwell for ever
The kings of the sea."

But, children, at midnight,
When soft the winds blow,
When clear falls the moonlight,
When spring tides are low;
When sweet airs come seaward
From heaths starred with broom,
And high rocks throw mildly
On the blanched sands a gloom;
Up the still, glistening beaches,
Up the creeks we will hie,
Over banks of bright seaweed
The ebb-tide leaves dry.
We will gaze, from the sand-hills,
At the white, sleeping town;
At the church on the hill-side—
And then come back down,
Singing: "There dwells a loved one,
But cruel is she!
She left lonely for ever
The kings of the sea."

Matthew Arnold

THE BLIND BEGGAR'S DAUGHTER
OF BEDNALL-GREEN

I T WAS A BLIND BEGGAR, had long lost his sight,
He had a fair daughter of beauty most bright;
And many a gallant brave suitor had she,
For none was so comely as pretty Bessee.

And though she was of favour most faire,
Yet seeing she was but a poor beggar's heyre,
Of ancyent housekeepers despisèd was she,
Whose sons came as suitors to pretty Bessee.

Wherefore in great sorrow fair Bessy did say,
"Good father, and mother, let me go away
To seek out my fortune, whatever it be."
This suit then they granted to pretty Bessee.

Then Bessy, that was of beauty so bright,
All clad in grey russet, and late in the night,
From father and mother alone parted she;
Who sighèd and sobbèd for pretty Bessee.

She went till she came to Stratford-le-Bow;
Then knew she not whither, nor which way to go:
With tears she lamented her hard destinie,
So sad and so heavy was pretty Bessee.

She kept on her journey until it was day,
She went unto Rumford along the high way;
Where at the Queen's Arms entertainèd was she:
So fair and well favoured was pretty Bessee.

Great gifts they did send her of silver and gold,
And in their songs daily her love was extoll'd;
Her beauty was blazèd in every degree;
So fair and so comely was pretty Bessee.

Four suitors at once unto her did go;
They cravèd her favour, but still she said, "No;
I would not wish gentles to marry with me."—
Yet ever they honoured pretty Bessee.

The first of them was a gallant young knight,
And he came unto her disguised in the night;
The second a gentleman of good degree,
Who wooèd and suèd for pretty Bessee.

A merchant of London, whose wealth was not small,
He was the third suitor, and proper withal:
Her master's own son the fourth man must be,
Who swore he would die for pretty Bessee.

"And, if thou wilt marry with me," quoth the knight,
I'll make thee a lady with joy and delight;
My heart so enthralled is by thy beautìe,
That soon I shall die for pretty Bessee."

The gentleman said, "Come, marry with me,
As fine as a lady my Bessy shall be:
My life is distressed: O hear me," quoth he;
"And grant me thy love, my pretty Bessee."—

"Let me be thy husband," the merchant did say,
"Thou shalt live in London, both gallant and gay;
My ships shall bring home rich jewels for thee,
And I will for ever love pretty Bessee."

Then Bessy she sighed, and thus she did say,
"My father and mother I mean to obey;
First get their good will, and be faithful to me,
And then you shall marry your pretty Bessee."

To every one this answer she made,
Wherefore unto her they joyfully said,
"This thing to fulfil we all do agree;
But where dwells thy father, my pretty Bessee?"

"My father," she said, "is soon to be seen:
The silly blind beggar of Bednall-green,
That daily sits begging for charitìe,
He is the good father of pretty Bessee.

"His marks and his tokens are known very well;
He always is led with a dog and a bell:
A silly old man, God knoweth, is he,
Yet he is the father of pretty Bessee."

"Nay then," quoth the merchant, "thou art not for me!"
"Nor," quoth the innholder, "my wife thou shalt be."
"I lothe," said the gentle, " a beggar's degree,
And therefore adieu, my pretty Bessee!"

"Why then," quoth the knight, "hap better or worse,
I weigh not true love by the weight of the purse,
And beauty is beauty in every degree;
Then welcome unto me, my pretty Bessee.

"With thee to thy father forthwith I will go."—
"Nay soft," quoth his kinsmen, "it must not be so;
A poor beggar's daughter no lady shall be,
Then take thy adieu of pretty Bessee."

But soon after this, by break of the day
The Knight had from Rumford stole Bessy away.
The young men of Rumford, as thick as might be,
Rode after to fetch again pretty Bessee.

As swift as the wind to ryde they were seen,
Until they came near unto Bednall-green;
And as the Knight lighted most courteouslìe,
They all fought against him for pretty Bessee.

But rescue came speedily over the plain,
Or else the young Knight for his love had been slain.
This fray being ended, then straightway he see
His kinsmen come railing at pretty Bessee.

Then spake the blind beggar, "Although I be poor,
Yet rail not against my child at my own door;
Though she be not deckèd in velvet and pearl,
Yet will I drop angels with you for my girl.

"And then, if my gold may better her birth,
And equal the gold that you lay on the earth,
Then neither rail nor grudge you to see
The blind beggar's daughter a lady to be.

"But first you shall promise, and have it well known,
The gold that you dropt shall all be your own."
With that they replied, "Contented be we."
"Then here's," quoth the beggar, "for pretty Bessee!"

With that an angel he cast on the ground,
And dropped in angels full three thousand pound,
And oftentimes it was provèd most plain,
For the gentlemen's one the beggar dropt twain:

So that the place, wherein they did sit,
With gold it was coverèd every whit.
The gentlemen then, having dropt all their store,
Said, "Now, beggar, hold, for we have no more,

"Thou hast fulfilled thy promise aright."—
"Then marry," quoth he, "my girl to this Knight;
And here," added he, "I will now throw you down
A hundred pounds more to buy her a gown."

The gentlemen all, that this treasure had seen,
Admirèd the beggar of Bednall-green:
And all those, that were her suitors before,
Their flesh for very anger they tore.

Thus was fair Bessy match'd to the Knight,
And then made a lady in others' despite:
A fairer lady there never was seen
Than the blind beggar's daughter of Bednall-green.

An Old Ballad

THE WARRIOR MAID

THEY BADE ME to my spinning
Because I was a maid,
But down into the battle
I marshalled unafraid.

Brightly against the sunbeams
I shook the flaming lance.
Then out I swept to gather
With the red and royal dance.

The war was stately in me,
And in my heart was pride—
Fierce moods like neighing horses
Most terribly did ride.

Deep as a sea of scarlet
I saw the banners roll—
And then the great war terror
Laid hold upon my soul.

I laughed aloud to feel it
And royally did cheer:
I strode amid my tremblings
And did not fear to fear.

A warrior rode against me.
I laid him to his rest.
I could not stop to gather
The bright sword from his breast.

But on I drove in splendor,
I—that was but a maid—
With piercing calls of triumph
And I was not afraid.

But once, beneath my charging,
A face shone up below.
Dead in the bloody furrow,
A stranger white as snow!

The foe rode close behind me!
I lost the day for this—
I sprang from off my stallion
And left on him a kiss.

The sword that pierced his bosom
With jewelled splendor shone.
I snatched it from him bleeding,
And lo, it was my own.

The spears blazed thick around me
When I leaped forth again.
But jubilant they found me
To face a thousand men.

Bright-voiced was my laughter,
I—that was but a maid!
And when the sharp gyve bound me,
Then was I not afraid.

Ah, hadst thou lived, my warrior,
Among the glorious ones,
I had borne thee savage daughters
And beautiful fierce sons.

Anna Hempstead Branch

YOUNG BEICHAN

IN LONDON was young Beichan born,
    He longed strange countries for to see,
But he was ta'en by a savage Moor,
    Who handled him right cruellie.

For he viewed the fashions of that land,
    Their way of worship viewèd he,
But to Mahound or Termagant
    Would Beichan never bend a knee.

So in every shoulder they've putten a bore,
    In every bore they've putten a tree,
And they have made him trail the wine
    And spices on his fair bodie.

They've casten him in a dungeon deep,
    Where he could neither hear nor see,
For seven years they've kept him there,
    Till he for hunger's like to dee.

This Moor he had but ae daughter,
  Her name was called Susie Pye,
And every day as she took the air,
  Near Beichan's prison she passed by.

And so it fell upon a day,
  About the middle time of Spring,
As she was passing by that way,
  She heard young Beichan sadly sing.

All night long no rest she got,
  Young Beichan's song for thinking on;
She's stown the keys from her father's head,
  And to the prison strang is gone.

And she has opened the prison doors,
  I wot she opened two or three,
Ere she could come young Beichan at,
  He was locked up so curiouslie.

But when she cam' young Beichan till,
  Sore wondered he that may to see;
He took her for some fair captive:
  "Fair lady, I pray, of what countrie?"

"O have ye any lands," she said,
  "Or castles in your own countrie,
That ye could give to a lady fair,
  From prison strang to set you free?"

"Near London town I have a hall,
   And other castles two or three;
I'll give them all to the lady fair
   That out of prison will set me free."

"Give me the truth of your right hand,
   The truth of it give unto me,
That for seven years ye'll no lady wed,
   Unless it be alang with me."

"I'll give thee the truth of my right hand,
   The truth of it I'll freely gie,
That for seven years I'll stay unwed,
   For the kindness thou dost show to me."

And she has brib'd the proud warder,
   Wi' mickle gold and white monie,
She's gotten the keys of the prison strang,
   And she has set young Beichan free.

She's gi'en him to eat the good spice-cake,
   She's gi'en him to drink the blude-red wine,
She's bidden him sometimes think on her,
   That sae kindly freed him out o' pine.

And she has broken her finger-ring,
   And to Beichan half of it gave she:
"Keep it, to mind you in foreign land
   Of the lady's love that set you free.

"And set your foot on good ship-board,
   And haste ye back to your ain countrie,
And before that seven years have an end,
   Come back again, love, and marry me."

But lang ere seven years had an end,
   She longed full sore her love to see,
So she's set her foot on good ship-board,
   And turned her back on her ain countrie.

She sailèd east, she sailèd west,
   Till to fair England's shore she came,
Where a bonny shepherd she espied,
   Was feeding his sheep upon the plain.

"What news, what news, thou bonny shepherd?
   What news hast thou to tell to me?"
"Such news I hear, ladie," he says,
   "The like was never in this countrie.

"There is a wedding in yonder hall,
   And ever the bells ring merrilie;
It is Lord Beichan's wedding-day
   Wi' a lady fair o' high degree."

She's putten her hand into her pocket,
   Gi'en him the gold and white monie;
"Hay, take ye that, my bonny boy,
   All for the news thou tell'st to me."

When she came to young Beichan's gate,
   She tirlèd saftly at the pin;
So ready was the proud porter
   To open and let this lady in.

"Is this young Beichan's hall," she said,
   "Or is that noble lord within?"
"Yea, he's in the hall among them all,
   And this is the day o' his weddin'."

"And has he wed anither love?
   And has he clean forgotten me?"
And sighing said that ladie gay,
   "I wish I were in my ain countrie."

And she has ta'en her gay gold ring
   That with her love she brake sae free;
Says, "Gie him that, ye proud porter,
   And bid the bridegroom speak wi' me.'

When the porter came his lord before,
   He kneeled down low upon his knee:
"What aileth thee, my proud porter,
   Thou art so full of courtesie?"

"I've been porter at your gates,
   It's now for thirty years and three;
But the lovely lady that stands thereat,
   The like o' her did I never see.

"For on every finger she has a ring,
    And on her mid-finger she has three,
And meikle gold aboon her brow.
    Sae fair a may did I never see."

It's out then spak the bride's mother,
    And an angry woman, I wot, was she:
"Ye might have excepted our bonny bride,
    And twa or three of our companie."

"O hold your tongue, thou bride's mother,
    Of all your folly let me be;
She's ten times fairer nor the bride,
    And all that's in your companie.

"And this golden ring that's broken in twa,
    This half o' a golden ring sends she:
'Ye'll carry that to Lord Beichan,' she says,
    'And bid him come an' speak wi' me.'

"She begs one sheave of your white bread,
    But and a cup of your red wine,
And to remember the lady's love
    That last relieved you out of pine."

"O well-a-day!" said Beichan then,
    "That I so soon have married me!
For it can be none but Susie Pye,
    That for my love has sailed the sea."

And quickly hied he down the stair;
    Of fifteen steps he made but three;
He's ta'en his bonny love in his arms
    And kist and kist her tenderlie.

"O hae ye ta'en anither bride?
    And hae ye clean forgotten me?
And hae ye quite forgotten her
    That gave you life and libertie?"

She lookit o'er her left shoulder,
    To hide the tears stood in her ee:
"Now fare thee well, young Beichan," she says,
    "I'll try to think no more on thee."

"O never, never, Susie Pye,
    For surely this can never be,
Nor ever shall I wed but her
    That's done and dreed so much for me."

Then out and spak the forenoon bride:
    "My lord, your love it changeth soon.
This morning I was made your bride,
    And another chose ere it be noon."

"O hold thy tongue, thou forenoon bride,
    Ye're ne'er a whit the worse for me,
And whan ye return to your ain land,
    A double dower I'll send with thee."

He's ta'en Susie Pye by the milkwhite hand,
  And led her thro' the halls sae hie,
And aye as he kist her red-rose lips,
  "Ye're dearly welcome, jewel, to me."

He's ta'en her by the milkwhite hand,
  And led her to yon fountain-stane;
He's changed her name from Susie Pye,
  And call'd her his bonny love, Lady Jane.

An Old Ballad

COLOMEN

THE DOVES THAT COO in Colomen
Are never heard by mortal men
But when a human creature passes
Underneath the churchyard grasses.
In deep voices, velvet-warm,
They tell of ancient perils, storm
Long hushed, and hopes withered and dead,
And joys a long while harvested.

There was a lady small and thin
(Oh, grave! Why did you let her in?)
Her voice was sad as a dove's, her feet
Went softly through the yellow wheat,
Like stars that haunt the evening west.
Hers was the tall, round, sunny cote
Whence, as she called, her doves would float
Softly, on arm and shoulder rest,
Until the lady, leaning so,
Under the feathers of rose and snow,

Wing of azure and purple plume,
Was like a slim tree bent with bloom.

And still, at Colomen, they say,
When midsummer has stolen away
The last arch primrose, and swiftly fall
Hawthorn petals, wan as a pall,
And the grave blackbirds, that of late
Shouted the sun up, meditate,
You hear about the ruined cote
A mighty, muted sound of wings,
And faint, ghostly flutterings.
Then, if your death is near, you see
A lady standing like a tree
Bent down with blossom. Long ago
Her little joy, her long woe!

In an April dawn of rose and flame
A poor, travelling painter came
Through tasselled woods, and in the tower
Beheld the lady, like a flower—
A pale flower beneath the hill,
Trembling when the air is still,
Broken when the storms are wild.
The lady looked on him, and smiled.
Woe, woe to Colomen,
Where never lovers come again,
Laughing in the morning air!

Dew decked the lady's hair
Because the lilac, purple and tall,
Saw her beauty and let fall
All her silver, all her sweet.
In dove-grey dusk their lips would meet
In the room beneath the tower
Where the drowsy sunlight smote
Seldom, and the air would creep
Stealthily and half asleep,
While stillness held the dancing mote,
And croonings fell from the ivied cote
With a musical, low roar,
Like summer seas on a fairy shore.

The boding wind had moaned of loss;
The boding shadow laid a cross
From the barred window to their feet;
The doves made a heart-broken, sweet
Clamour of some eerie thing.
They did not hear nor understand
How soon love is withered away
Like a flower on a frosty day!

Early in a summer dawn
When the shadows of the doves were drawn
Down the roof, and from the clover
The bees' low roar came up, her lover
Finished her portrait, thin and small

And pale, with an ethereal
Sweet air, because he had seen her soul
Come to the threshold when she stole
To meet him. There forever she stood
Like a silver fairy in a wood
Or a maytree in the moonlight.
He told her of his dream's delight,
How they would dwell alone, aloof,
With doves crooning on the roof.

He had painted through a sapphire June
Into a thunderous dark July.
Alas! How fleet is spring! How soon
From all their little windows fly
The doves of joy! In an evil hour
Her sister saw him leave the tower.

For all her simple country grace,
Hers was a haughty, lordly race.
When night was thick and black above,
They sent the press-gang for her love.

All day, beside the memoried cote
She lay so still they thought her dead,
Her doves, that wheeled above her head.
But in her eyes a wild, remote,
Inhuman sorrow slumbered.

When next the clover called the bee,
Where was she? Ah, where was she?
She dragged her laden limbs across
The grey lawns, to hear the sound
That turned a sword within her wound
And made her agony of loss
So keen that if she held her breath
She almost heard the feet of death.

When all her thronging pigeons cooed
Around, with outspread arms she stood.
She seemed a pale and slender tree,
Bent with snow and not with bloom—
Bent lower towards the tomb.

She would be free of the distress
That men call joy, the littleness
That men call life—as birds are free.
So in the dewy morning hour
She hanged herself within the tower,
Beside her portrait, spirit-fair,
With these words written: 'We come again,
And ours the house of Colomen.'

Her cousins came and found her there,
While high against the painted dawn
Her pigeons—rosy, white and fawn,
Coal-black and mottled—wheeled in the air.
But while they gazed, weeping aloud,
Around the tower a silence fell.
The doves wheeled high: they could not tell
Which were birds and which was cloud.

A haunted silence held the tower,
Wherein the portrait's living eyes
Watched the dead lady with surprise,
Like a flower that gazes on a flower.

No doves returned there evermore.
The spiders wove about the door
Intricate tapestries of time,
That held the dew and held the rime.
And from the house of Colomen,
Like water from a frozen strand,
Failed the voices of maids and men,
Shrivelled the heart, shrivelled the hand,
Till there within the arching wood
No face was left but the painted face,
No sound was left of the human race,
But only the sound of doves that cooed
Sadly, intermittently—
Wheeling doves that none can see

But dying men who wander here
And see a picture, glassy-clear,
Where the milky hawthorn-blossom falls
And from the elm a blackbird calls:

Then softly from the ruined cote
A pigeon coos—and faint, remote,
A hundred pigeons answer low,
Voicing the lady's ancient woe;
And then they see her, very fair
And fragile in the scented air;
On arms and shoulders doves alight,
Multiple-tinted, like a bright
Tapestry that time has faded.
Softly purple, lilac-shaded,
The lady standeth, like a tree
Bent down with blossom. . . .

Mary Webb

GREEN BROOM

THERE WAS AN OLD MAN lived out in the wood,
 His trade was a-cutting of Broom, green Broom;
He had but one son without thrift, without good,
 Who lay in his bed till 'twas noon, bright noon.

The old man awoke, one morning and spoke,
 He swore he would fire the room, that room,
If his John would not rise and open his eyes,
 And away to the wood to cut Broom, green Broom.

So Johnny arose, and he slipped on his clothes,
 And away to the wood to cut Broom, green Broom,
He sharpened his knives, for once he contrives
 To cut a great bundle of Broom, green Broom.

When Johnny passed under a lady's fine house,
 Passed under a lady's fine room, fine room,
She called to her maid, "Go fetch me," she said,
 "Go fetch me the boy that sells Broom, green Broom."

When Johnny came in to the lady's fine house,
    And stood in the lady's fine room, fine room;
"Young Johnny," she said, "Will you give up your trade,
    And marry a lady in bloom, full bloom?"

Johnny gave his consent, and to church they both went,
    And he wedded the lady in bloom, full bloom,
At market and fair, all folks do declare,
    There is none like the Boy that sold Broom, green Broom.

An Old Ballad

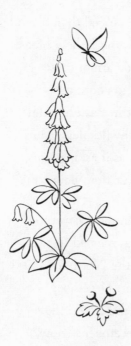

THE SKELETON IN ARMOR

SPEAK! SPEAK! thou fearful guest!
Who, with thy hollow breast
Still in rude armor drest,
    Comest to daunt me!
Wrapt not in Eastern balms,
But with thy fleshless palms
Stretched, as if asking alms,
    Why dost thou haunt me?"

Then, from those cavernous eyes
Pale flashes seemed to rise,
As when the Northern skies
    Gleam in December;
And, like the water's flow
Under December's snow,
Came a dull voice of woe
    From the heart's chamber.

"I was a Viking old!
My deeds, though manifold,
No Skald in song has told,
    No Saga taught thee!
Take heed that in thy verse
Thou dost the tale rehearse,
Else dread a dead man's curse;
    For this I sought thee.

"Far in the Northern Land,
By the wild Baltic's strand,
I, with my childish hand,
    Tamed the gerfalcon;
And, with my skates fast-bound,
Skimmed the half-frozen Sound,
That the poor whimpering hound
    Trembled to walk on.

"Oft to his frozen lair
Tracked I the grisly bear,
While from my path the hare
    Fled like a shadow;
Oft through the forest dark
Followed the were-wolf's bark,
Until the soaring lark
    Sang from the meadow.

"But when I older grew,
Joining a corsair's crew,
O'er the dark sea I flew
 With the marauders.
Wild was the life we led;
Many the souls that sped,
Many the hearts that bled,
 By our stern orders.

"Many a wassail-bout
Wore the long Winter out;
Often our midnight shout
 Set the cocks crowing,
As we the Berserk's tale
Measured in cups of ale,
Draining the oaken pail
 Filled to o'erflowing.

"Once as I told in glee
Tales of the stormy sea,
Soft eyes did gaze on me,
 Burning yet tender;
And as the white stars shine
On the dark Norway pine,
On that dark heart of mine
 Fell their soft splendor.

"I wooed the blue-eyed maid,
Yielding, yet half afraid,
And in the forest's shade
   Our vows were plighted.
Under its loosened vest
Fluttered her little breast,
Like birds within their nest
   By the hawk frighted.

"Bright in her father's hall
Shields gleamed upon the wall,
Loud sang the minstrels all
   Chanting his glory;
When of old Hildebrand
I asked his daughter's hand,
Mute did the minstrels stand
   To hear my story.

"While the brown ale he quaffed,
Loud then the champion laughed,
And as the wind-gusts waft
   The sea-foam brightly,
So the loud laugh of scorn,
Out of those lips unshorn,
From the deep drinking-horn
   Blew the foam lightly.

"She was a Prince's child,
I but a Viking wild,
And though she blushed and smiled,
    I was discarded!
Should not the dove so white
Follow the sea-mew's flight?
Why did they leave that night
    Her nest unguarded?

"Scarce had I put to sea,
Bearing the maid with me,—
Fairest of all was she
    Among the Norsemen!—
When on the white sea-strand,
Waving his armèd hand,
Saw we old Hildebrand,
    With twenty horsemen.

"Then launched they to the blast,
Bent like a reed each mast,
Yet we were gaining fast,
    When the wind failed us;
And with a sudden flaw
Came round the gusty Skaw,
So that our foe we saw
    Laugh as he hailed us.

"And as to catch the gale
Round veered the flapping sail,
'Death!' was the helmsman's hail,
    'Death without quarter!'
Midships with iron keel
Struck we her ribs of steel;
Down her black hulk did reel
    Through the black water!

"As with his wings aslant,
Sails the fierce cormorant,
Seeking some rocky haunt,
    With his prey laden,—
So toward the open main,
Beating to sea again,
Through the wild hurricane,
    Bore I the maiden.

"Three weeks we westward bore,
And when the storm was o'er,
Cloud-like we saw the shore
    Stretching to leeward;
There for my lady's bower
Built I the lofty tower
Which, to this very hour,
    Stands looking seaward.

"There lived we many years;
Time dried the maiden's tears;
She had forgot her fears,
   She was a mother;
Death closed her mild blue eyes;
Under that tower she lies;
Ne'er shall the sun arise
   On such another.

"Still grew my bosom then,
Still as a stagnant fen!
Hateful to me were men,
   The sunlight hateful!
In the vast forest here,
Clad in my warlike gear,
Fell I upon my spear,
   Oh, death was grateful!

"Thus, seamed with many scars,
Bursting these prison bars,
Up to its native stars
   My soul ascended!
There from the flowing bowl
Deep drinks the warrior's soul,
Skoal! to the Northland! *skoal!*"
   Thus the tale ended.

Henry Wadsworth Longfellow

THE FAIR FLOWER
OF NORTHUMBERLAND

I

T WAS A KNIGHT in Scotland born,
  Follow, my love, come over the strand—
Was taken prisoner and left forlorn,
  Even by the good Earl of Northumberland.

Then was he cast in prison strong,
  Follow, my love, come over the strand—
Where he could not walk nor lie along,
  Even by the good Earl of Northumberland.

And as in sorrow thus he lay,
  Follow, my love, come over the strand—
The Earl's sweet daughter walk'd that way,
  And she the faire flower of Northumberland.

And loud to her this knight did crie,
  Follow, my love, come over the strand—
The salt teares standing in his eye,
  And she the faire flower of Northumberland.

"Faire lady," he said, "take pity on me,
  Follow, my love, come over the strand—
And let me not in prison dee,
  And you the faire flower of Northumberland,"—

"Faire sir, how should I take pity on thee?
  Follow, my love, come over the strand—
Thou being a foe to our countrie,
  And I the faire flower of Northumberland."

"Faire lady, I am no foe," he said,
  Follow, my love, come over the strand—
Through thy sweet love here was I stay'd,
  For thee, the faire flower of Northumberland."—

"Why shouldst thou come here for love of me,
  Follow, my love, come over the strand—
Having wife and children in thy countrie?
  —And I the faire flower of Northumberland."—

"I swear by the blessèd Trinitie,
  Follow, my love, come over the strand—
I have no wife nor children, I,
  But I'll make you my ladye in faire Scotland.

"I swear by Him that was crown'd with thorn,
  Follow, my love, come over the strand—
That I never had wife since the day I was born,
  But I live a free lord in faire Scotland."—

She stole from her father's pillow the key,
  Follow, my love, come over the strand—
And soon out of prison she's set him free
  To wend with her into faire Scotland.

Likewise much gold she got by sleight,
  Follow, my love, come over the strand—
And all to help this forlorne knight
  To wend from her father to faire Scotland.

She's led him down to her father's stable,
  Follow, my love, come over the strand—
And she's stolen two steeds both wight and able,
  To carry them on to faire Scotland.

They rode till they came to water clear,
  Follow, my love, come over the strand—
"Good Sir, how should I follow you here,
  And I the faire flower of Northumberland?

"The water is rough and wonderful steepe,
  Follow, my love, come over the strand—
And on my saddle I shall not keepe,
  And I the faire flower of Northumberland."—

"Fear not the ford, faire lady," quoth he,
  Follow, my love, come over the strand—
For long I cannot stay for thee,
  And thou the faire flower of Northumberland."

From top to toe all wet was she:

Follow, my love, come over the strand—

"This have I done for love of thee,

And I the faire flower of Northumberland."

They rode till they came to a Scottish moss,

Follow, my love, come over the strand—

He bade her light off from her father's horse,

Says, "Go get you back to Northumberland."

"For I have a wife and children five,

Follow, my love, come over the strand—

In Edenborrow they be alive,

So get thee home to Northumberland."—

"Have pity on me as I had on thee!

Follow, my love, come over the strand—

A cook in your kitchen I will be,

Even I, the faire flower of Northumberland."

"Or take me by the body so meek,

Follow, my love, come over the strand—

And throw me in the water so deep,

For I darena go back to Northumberland."

He turn'd him around and he thought of a plan,

Follow, my love, come over the strand—

He bought an old horse and he hired an old man

To carry her back to Northumberland.

When she came thro' her father's ha',
Follow, my love, come over the strand—
She louted her low amongst them a',
She was the faire flower of Northumberland.

Down came her father, he saw her and smiled,
Follow, my love, come over the strand—
"You arena the first the false Scots have beguiled,
And ye're aye welcome back to Northumberland!"

An Old Ballad

THE HIGHWAYMAN

THE WIND was a torrent of darkness among the gusty trees
The moon was a ghostly galleon tossed upon cloudy seas,
The road was a ribbon of moonlight over the purple moor,
And the highwayman came riding—
   Riding—riding—
The highwayman came riding, up to the old inn-door.

He'd a French cocked-hat on his forehead, a bunch of lace
   at his chin,
A coat of the claret velvet, and breeches of brown doe-skin
They fitted with never a wrinkle: his boots were up to th
   thigh!
And he rode with a jeweled twinkle,
   His pistol butts a-twinkle,
His rapier hilt a-twinkle, under the jeweled sky.

Over the cobbles he clattered and clashed in the dar
   inn-yard,

nd he tapped with his whip on the shutters, but all was
    locked and barred;
Ie whistled a tune to the window, and who should be wait-
    ing there
ut the landlord's black-eyed daughter,
    Bess, the landlord's daughter,
aiting a dark red love-knot into her long black hair.

nd dark in the dark old inn-yard a stable-wicket creaked
/here Tim the ostler listened; his face was white and
    peaked;
is eyes were hollows of madness, his hair like mouldy hay,
ıt he loved the landlord's daughter,
    The landlord's red-lipped daughter,
umb as a dog he listened, and he heard the robber say—

)ne kiss, my bonny sweetheart, I'm after a prize tonight,
ıt I shall be back with the yellow gold before the morning
    light;
:t, if they press me sharply, and harry me through the day,
hen look for me by moonlight,
    Watch for me by moonlight,
l come to thee by moonlight, though hell should bar the
    way."

e rose upright in the stirrups; he scarce could reach her
    hand,
ıt she loosened her hair i' the casement! His face burnt
    like a brand

As the black cascade of perfume came tumbling over h
    breast!
And he kissed its waves in the moonlight,
    (Oh, sweet black waves in the moonlight!)
Then he tugged at his rein in the moonlight, and gallope
    away to the West.

He did not come in the dawning; he did not come at noo
And out o' the tawny sunset, before the rise o' the moon,
When the road was a gipsy's ribbon, looping the purple moo
A red-coat troop came marching—
    Marching—marching—
King George's men came marching, up to the old inn-door.

They said no word to the landlord, they drank his ale instea
But they gagged his daughter and bound her to the foot
    her narrow bed;
Two of them knelt at her casement, with muskets at the
    side!
There was death at every window;
    And hell at one dark window;
For Bess could see, through her casement, the road that
    would ride.

They had tied her up to attention, with many a sniggeri
    jest;

58

They had bound a musket beside her, with the barrel beneath
    her breast!
"Now keep good watch!" and they kissed her.
   She heard the dead man say—
Look for me by moonlight;
   Watch for me by moonlight;
I'll come to thee by moonlight, though hell should bar th
    way!

She twisted her hands behind her; but all the knots hel
    good!
She writhed her hands till her fingers were wet with sweat
    blood!
They stretched and strained in the darkness, and the hou
    crawled by like years,
Till, now, on the stroke of midnight,
   Cold, on the stroke of midnight,
The tip of one finger touched it! The trigger at least was he

The tip of one finger touched it; she strove no more for t
    rest!
Up, she stood up to attention, with the barrel beneath h
    breast,
She would not risk their hearing; she would not strive agai
For the road lay bare in the moonlight;
   Blank and bare in the moonlight;
And the blood of her veins in the moonlight throbbed to h
    love's refrain.

lot-tlot; tlot-tlot! Had they heard it? The horse-hoofs ring-
   ing clear;
lot-tlot, tlot-tlot, in the distance? Were they deaf that they
   did not hear?
own the ribbon of moonlight, over the brow of the hill,
he highwayman came riding,
   Riding, riding!
he red-coats looked to their priming! She stood up, straight
   and still!

lot-tlot, in the frosty silence! *Tlot-tlot,* in the echoing night!
earer he came and nearer! Her face was like a light!
er eyes grew wide for a moment; she drew one last deep
   breath,
hen her finger moved in the moonlight,
   Her musket shattered the moonlight,
attered her breast in the moonlight and warned him—with
   her death.

e turned; he spurred to the West; he did not know who
   stood
wed, with her head o'er the musket, drenched with her
   own red blood!
ot till the dawn he heard it, his face grew grey to hear
ow Bess, the landlord's daughter,
   The landlord's black-eyed daughter,
ad watched for her love in the moonlight, and died in the
   darkness there.

Back, he spurred like a madman, shrieking a curse to the sk

With the white road smoking behind him and his rapie
brandished high!

Blood-red were his spurs i' the golden noon: wine-red wa
his velvet coat,

When they shot him down on the highway,
Down like a dog in the highway,

And he lay in his blood on the highway, with the bunc
of lace at his throat.

And still of a winter's night, they say, when the wind is
the trees,

When the moon is a ghostly galleon tossed upon cloudy sea

When the road is a ribbon of moonlight over the purple moc

A highwayman comes riding—
Riding—riding—

A highwayman comes riding, up to the old inn-door.

Over the cobbles he clatters and clangs in the dark inn-yar

He taps with his whip on the shutters, but all is locked ar
barred;

He whistles a tune to the window, and who should be waitir
there

But the landlord's black-eyed daughter,
Bess, the landlord's daughter,

Plaiting a dark red love-knot into her long black hair.

Alfred Noy

THE CRUEL BROTHER

THERE WERE THREE LADIES play'd at the ba',
  With a hey ho! and a lily gay!
By came a knight and he woo'd them a'
  As the primrose spreads so sweetly.
    Sing Annet, and Marret, and fair Maisrie,
    As the dew hangs i' the wood, gay ladie!

The first ane she was clad in red:
"O lady fair, will you be my bride?"

The midmost ane was clad in green:
"O lady fair, will you be my queen?"

The youngest o' them was clad in white:
"O lady fair, be my heart's delight!"

"Sir knight, ere ye my favour win,
Ye maun get consent frae a' my kin.

"Ye maun go ask my father, the King:
Sae maun ye ask my mither, the Queen.

"Sae maun ye ask my sister Anne,
And dinna forget my brother John."

He has sought her from her father, the King
And sae did he her mither, the Queen.

He has sought her from her sister Anne:
But he has forgot her brither John.

Now when the wedding day was come,
The knight would take his bonny bride home.

And many a lord and many a knight
Came to behold that ladie bright.

And there was nae man that did her see
But wish'd himself bridegroom to be.

Her father led her down the stair,
And her mither dear she kiss'd her there.

Her sister Anne led her thro' the close,
And her brother John set her on her horse.

She lean'd her o'er the saddle-bow,
To give him a kiss ere she did go.

He has ta'en a knife, baith lang and sharp,
And stabb'd that bonny bride to the heart.

She hadna ridden half thro' the town,
Until her heart's blude stain'd her gown.

"Ride saftly up," said the best young man;
I think our bride come hooly on."

"Ride up, ride up," said the second man;
I think our bride looks pale and wan."

Up then comes the gay bridegroom,
And straight unto the bride he came.

"Does your side-saddle sit awry?
Or does your steed go heavily?"

"O lead me gently over yon stile,
For there would I sit and bleed awhile.

"O lead me gently up yon hill,
For there I would sit and make my will."

"O what will you leave to your father dear?"
"The milk-white steed that brought me here."

"What will you leave to your mother dear?"
"My wedding shift that I do wear."

"What will you leave to your sister Anne?"
"My silken snood and my golden fan."

"What will you leave to your brother John?"
With a hey ho! and a lily gay!
"The gallows-tree to hang him on."
And the primrose spreads so sweetly.
Sing Annet, and Marret, and fair Maisrie,
And the dew hangs i' the wood, gay ladie!

An Old Ballad

LA BELLE DAME SANS MERCI

O, WHAT CAN AIL THEE, knight at arms,
    Alone and palely loitering;
The sedge has withered from the lake,
    And no birds sing.

O, what can ail thee, knight at arms,
    So haggard and so woe-begone?
The squirrel's granary is full,
    And the harvest's done.

I see a lily on thy brow
    With anguish moist and fever-dew,
And on thy cheeks a fading rose
    Fast withereth too.

I met a lady in the meads,
    Full beautiful—a faery's child,
Her hair was long, her foot was light,
    And her eyes were wild.

I made a garland for her head,
    And bracelets too, and fragrant zone,
She looked at me as she did love,
    And made sweet moan.

I set her on my pacing steed
    And nothing else saw all day long;
For sideways would she lean, and sing
    A faery's song.

She found me roots of relish sweet,
    And honey wild and manna dew;
And sure in language strange she said—
    I love thee true.

She took me to her elfin grot,
    And there she gazed and sighed full sore:
And there I shut her wild wild eyes
    With kisses four.

And there she lullèd me asleep,
    And there I dreamed, ah woe betide,
The latest dream I ever dreamed
    On the cold hill side.

I saw pale kings and princes too,
    Pale warriors, death-pale were they all:
They cry'd—"La belle Dame sans Merci
    Hath thee in thrall!"

I saw their starved lips in the gloam
  With horrid warning gapèd wide,
And I awoke, and found me here
  On the cold hill side.

And this is why I sojourn here
  Alone and palely loitering,
Though the sedge is withered from the lake,
  And no birds sing.

John Keats

YOUNG CHARLOTTE

Young charlotte lived on the mountain side
   In a lone and dreary spot;
No other house for miles around
   Except her father's cot.

And yet on many a winter's night,
   Young swains were gathered there;
For her father kept a social board,
   And she was very fair.

Her father loved to see her dressed
   Like any city belle;
She was the only child he had
   And he loved his daughter well.

On New Year's eve as the sun went down,
   Far looked her wistful eye
Out from the frosty window pane
   As the merry sleighs passed by.

In the village fifteen miles away,
    Was to be a ball that night,
And though the air was piercing cold
    Her heart beat warm and light.

How brightly beams her laughing eye,
    As a well-known voice she hears;
And driving up to the cottage door
    Young Charles and his sleigh appears.

"O daughter dear," her mother said,
    "This blanket round you fold;
It is a dreadful night without,
    You'll catch your death of cold."

"O no, O no!" young Charlotte cried,
    And she laughed like a gypsy queen;
"To ride in blankets muffled up,
    I never will be seen.

"My silken cloak is quite enough,
    You know it's lined throughout;
Besides I have my silken scarf
    To tie my neck about."

Her bonnet and her gloves put on,
    She stepped into the sleigh,
Rode swiftly down the mountain side
    And o'er the hills away.

There was music in the sound of the bells,
    As o'er the hills they go;
Such a creaking noise the runners make
    As they cleave the frozen snow.

With muffled face and silent lips
    Five miles at length were passed
When Charles with few and shivering words
    The silence broke at last.

"Such a dreadful night I never knew,
    My reins I scarce can hold."
Fair Charlotte shivering faintly said,
    "I am exceeding cold."

He cracked his whip, he urged his steed
    Much faster than before.
And thus five other dreary miles
    In silence they passed o'er.

Says Charles, "How fast the freezing ice
    Is gathering on my brow."
And Charlotte still more faintly said,
    "I'm growing warmer now."

So on they rode through frosty air
    And the glittering cold starlight,
Until at last the village lamps
    And the ballroom came in sight.

Charles drove to the door, he then jumped out,
   And reached his hand for her.
Why sit there like a monument
   That has no power to stir?

He called her once, he called her twice;
   She answered not a word.
He asked her for her hand again,
   But still she never stirred.

He took her hand in his—O God!
   'Twas cold and hard as stone.
He tore the mantle from her brow
   Cold sweat upon there shone.

Then quickly to the dancing hall
   Her lifeless form he bore;
Fair Charlotte was a frozen corpse
   And spake she nevermore.

And then he sat down by her side
   While bitter tears did flow,
And cried, "My own, my charming bride,
   You never more will know."

He twined his arms around her neck
   And kissed her marble brow;
His thoughts flew back to where she said,
   "I'm growing warmer now."

'Twas then that cruel monster, Death,
  Had claimed her as his own;
Young Charlotte's eyes were closed for aye,
  Her voice was heard no more.

He carried her out to the sleigh,
  And with her he rode home;
And when he reached the cottage door
  O how her parents mourned.

Her parents mourned for their daughter dear,
  And Charles wept o'er the gloom.
Till at last young Charles too died of grief
  And they both lie in one tomb.

Young ladies, think of this fair girl
  And always dress aright,
And never venture thinly clad
  On such a wintry night.

An Old Ballad

THE SINGING LEAVES

WHAT FAIRINGS will ye that I bring?"
Said the King to his daughters three;
"For I to Vanity Fair am boun',
Now say what shall they be?"

Then up and spake the eldest daughter,
That lady tall and grand:
"O, bring me pearls and diamonds great,
And gold rings for my hand."

Thereafter spake the second daughter,
That was both white and red:
"For me bring silks that will stand alone,
And a gold comb for my head."

Then came the turn of the least daughter,
That was whiter than thistledown,
And among the gold of her blithesome hair
Dim shone the golden crown.

"There came a bird this morning,
    And sang 'neath my bower eaves,
Till I dreamed, as his music made me,
    'Ask thou for the Singing Leaves'."

Then the brow of the King swelled crimson
    With a flush of angry scorn:
"Well have ye spoken, my two eldest,
    And chosen as ye were born;

"But she, like a thing of peasant race,
    That is happy binding the sheaves";
Then he saw her dead mother in her face,
    And said, "Thou shalt have thy leaves."

He mounted and rode three days and nights
    Till he came to Vanity Fair,
And 'twas easy to buy the gems and the silk,
    But no Singing Leaves were there.

Then deep in the greenwood rode he,
    And asked of every tree,
"O, if you have ever a Singing Leaf,
    I pray you give it me!"

But the trees all kept their counsel,
    And never a word said they,
Only there sighed from the pine tops
    A music of seas far away.

Only the pattering aspen
    Made a sound of growing rain,
That fell ever faster and faster,
    Then faltered to silence again.

"O, where shall I find a little foot-page
    That would win both hose and shoon,
And will bring to me the Singing Leaves
    If they grow under the moon?"

Then lightly turned him Walter the page,
    By the stirrup as he ran:
"Now pledge you me the truesome word
    Of a king and gentleman,

"That you will give me the first, first thing
    You meet at your castle gate,
And the Princess shall get the Singing Leaves,
    Or mine be a traitor's fate."

The King's head dropt upon his breast
    A moment, as it might be;
'Twill be my dog, he thought, and said,
    "My faith I plight to thee."

Then Walter took from next his heart
  A packet small and thin,
"Now give you this to the Princess Anne,
  The Singing Leaves are therein."

As the King rode in at his castle gate,
  A maiden to meet him ran,
And "Welcome, Father!" she laughed and cried
  Together, the Princess Anne.

"Lo, here the Singing Leaves," quoth he,
  "And woe, but they cost me dear!"
She took the packet, and the smile
  Deepened down beneath the tear.

It deepened down till it reached her heart,
  And then gushed up again,
And lighted her tears as the sudden sun
  Transfigures the summer rain.

And the first Leaf, when it was opened,
  Sang: "I am Walter the page,
And the songs I sing 'neath thy window
  Are my only heritage."

And the second Leaf sang: "But in the land
   That is neither on earth or sea,
My lute and I are lords of more
   Than thrice this kingdom's fee."

And the third Leaf sang: "Be mine! Be mine!"
   And ever it sang, "Be mine!"
Then sweeter it sang and ever sweeter,
   And said, "I am thine, thine, thine!"

At the first Leaf she grew pale enough,
   At the second she turned aside,
At the third, 'twas as if a lily flushed
   With a rose's red heart's tide.

"Good counsel gave the bird," said she,
   "I have my hope thrice o'er,
For they sing to my very heart," she said,
   "And it sings to them evermore."

She brought to him her beauty and truth,
   But and broad earldoms three,
And he made her queen of the broader lands
   He held of his lute in fee.

James Russell Lowell

THE BAILIFF'S DAUGHTER
OF ISLINGTON

THERE WAS A YOUTH, and a well-beloved youth,
 And he was a squire's son:
He loved the bailiff's daughter dear,
 That lived in Islington.

Yet she was coy, and would not believe
 That he did love her so,
No nor at any time would she
 Any countenance to him show.

But when his friends did understand
 His fond and foolish mind,
They sent him up to fair London,
 An apprentice for to bind.

And when he had been seven long years,
 And never his love could see,—
"Many a tear have I shed for her sake,
 When she little thought of me."

Then all the maids of Islington
　　Went forth to sport and play,
All but the bailiff's daughter dear;
　　She secretly stole away.

She pulled off her gown of green,
　　And put on ragged attire,
And to fair London she would go
　　Her true love to enquire.

And as she went along the high road,
　　The weather being hot and dry,
She sat her down upon a green bank,
　　And her true love came riding by.

She started up, with a color soe red,
　　Catching hold of his bridle-rein;
"One penny, one penny, kind sir," she said,
　　"Will ease me of much pain."

"Before I give you one penny, sweet-heart,
　　Praye tell me where you were born."
"At Islington, kind sir," sayd she,
　　"Where I have had many a scorn."

"I prythee, sweet-heart, then tell to me,
　　O tell me, whether you know
The bailiff's daughter of Islington."
　　"She is dead, sir, long ago."

"If she be dead, then take my horse,
   My saddle and bridle also;
For I will into some far country,
   Where no man shall me know."

"O stay, O stay, thou goodly youth,
   She standeth by thy side;
She is here alive, she is not dead,
   And ready to be thy bride."

"O farewell grief, and welcome joy,
   Ten thousand times therefore;
For now I have founde mine own true love,
   Whom I thought I should never see more."

An Old Ballad

THE EARL O' QUARTERDECK

THE WIND IT BLEW, and the ship it flew;
  And it was "Hey for hame!
And ho for hame!" But the skipper cried,
  "Haud her oot o'er the saut sea faem."

Then up and spoke the King himsel':
  "Haud on for Dunfermline!"
Quo the skipper, "Ye're king upon the land—
  I'm king upo' the brine."

And he took the helm intil his hand,
  And he steered the ship sae free;
Wi' the wind astarn, he crowded sail,
  And stood right out to sea.

Quo the king, "There's treason in this I vow;
  This is something underhand!
'Bout ship!" Quo the skipper, "Yer grace forgets
  Ye are king but o' the land!"

And still he held to the open sea;
    And the east-wind sank behind;
And the west had a bitter word to say,
    Wi' a white-sea roarin' wind.

And he turned her head into the north.
    Said the king: "Gar fling him o'er."
Quo the fearless skipper: "It's a' ye're worth!
    Ye'll ne'er see Scotland more."

The king crept down the cabin-stair,
    To drink the gude French wine.
And up she came, his daughter fair,
    And luikit ower the brine.

She turned her face to the drivin' hail,
    To the hail but and the weet;
Her snood it brak, and, as lang's hersel',
    Her hair drave out i' the sleet.

She turned her face frae the drivin' win'—
    "What's that ahead?" quo she.
The skipper he threw himsel' frae the win',
    And he drove the helm a-lee.

"Put to yer hand, my lady fair!
    Put to yer hand," quo he;
"Gin she dinna face the win' the mair,
    It's the waur for you and me."

For the skipper kenned that strength is strength,
    Whether woman's or man's at last.
To the tiller the lady she laid her han',
    And the ship laid her cheek to the blast.

For that slender body was full o' soul,
    And the will is mair than shape;
As the skipper saw when they cleared the berg,
    And he heard her quarter scrape.

Quo the skipper: "Ye are a lady fair,
    And a princess grand to see;
But ye are a woman, and a man wad sail
    To hell in yer company."

She liftit a pale and queenly face;
    Her een flashed, and syne they swim.
"And what for no to heaven?" she says,
    And she turned awa' frae him.

But she took na her han' frae the good ship's helm,
    Until the day did daw;
And the skipper he spak, but what he said
    It was said atween them twa.

And then the good ship she lay to,
    With the land far on the lee;
And up came the king upo' the deck,
    Wi' wan face and bluidshot ee.

The skipper he louted to the king:
   "Gae wa', gae wa'," said the king.
Said the king, like a prince, "I was a' wrang,
   Put on this ruby ring."

And the wind blew lowne, and the stars cam' oot,
   And the ship turned to the shore;
And, afore the sun was up again,
   They saw Scotland ance more.

That day the ship hung at the pier-heid,
   And the king he stept on the land.
"Skipper, kneel down," the king he said,
   "Hoo daur ye afore me stand?"

The skipper he louted on his knee,
   The king his blade he drew:
Said the king, "How daured ye contre me?
   I'm aboard my ain ship noo.

"I canna mak ye a king," said he,
   "For the Lord alone can do that;
And beside ye took it intil yer ain han'
   And crooned yersel' sae pat!

"But wi' what ye will I redeem my ring;
   For ance I am at your beck.
And first, as ye loutit Skipper o' Doon,
   Rise up Yerl o' Quarterdeck."

The skipper he rose and looked at the king
    In his een for all his croon;
Said the skipper, "Here is yer grace's ring,
    And yer daughter is my boon."

The reid blude sprang into the king's face,—
    A wrathful man to see:
"The rascal loon abuses our grace;
    Gae hang him upon yon tree."

But the skipper he sprang aboard his ship,
    And he drew his biding blade;
And he struck the chain that held her fast,
    But the iron was ower weel made.

And the king he blew a whistle loud;
    And tramp, tramp, down the pier,
Cam' twenty riders on twenty steeds,
    Clankin' wi' spur and spear.

"He saved your life!" cried the lady fair;
    "His life ye durna spill!"
"Will ye come atween me and my hate?"
    Quo the lady, "And that I will!"

And on cam' the knights wi' spur and spear,
    For they heard the iron ring.
"Gin ye care na for yer father's grace,
    Mind ye that I am the king."

"I kneel to my father for his grace,
Right lowly on my knee;
But I stand and look the king in the face,
For the skipper is king o' me."

She turned and she sprang upo' the deck,
And the cable splashed in the sea.
The good ship spread her wings sae white,
And away with the skipper goes she.

Now was not this a king's daughter,
And a brave lady beside?
And a woman with whom a man might sail
Into the heaven wi' pride?

George Macdonald

HYND HORN

Hynd horn's bound, love,
and Hynd Horn's free,
With a hey lillelu and a how lo lan;
Where was ye born, or in what countrie?
And the birk and the broom blows bonnie.

"In good greenwood, there I was born,
And all my forebears me beforn.

"O seven long years I served the King,
And as for wages I never gat nane;

"But ae sight o' his ae daughter.
And that was thro' an auger-bore."

Seven long years he served the King,
And it's a' for the sake of his daughter **Jean**.

The King an angry man was he;
He sent young Hynd Horn to the sea.

He's gi'en his luve a silver wand
Wi' seven silver laverocks sittin' thereon.

She's gi'en to him a gay gold ring
Wi' seven bright diamonds set therein.

"As lang's these diamonds keep their hue,
Ye'll know I am a lover true:

"But when the ring turns pale and wan,
Ye may ken that I love anither man."

He hoist up sails and awa' sail'd he
Till that he came to a foreign countrie.

One day as he look'd his ring upon,
He saw the diamonds pale and wan.

He's left the seas and he's come to the land,
And the first that he met was an auld beggar man.

"What news, what news? thou auld beggar man,
For it's seven years sin I've seen land."

"No news," said the beggar, "no news at a',
But there is a wedding in the King's ha'.

"But there is a wedding in the King's ha'
That has halden these forty days and twa'."

"Cast off, cast off thy auld beggar weed,
And I'll gi'e thee my gude grey steed:

"And lend to me your wig o' hair
To cover mine, because it is fair."

"My begging weed is na for thee,
Your riding steed is na for me."

But part by right and part by wrang
Hynd Horn has changed wi' the beggar man.

The auld beggar man was bound for to ride,
But young Hynd Horn was bound for the bride.

When he came to the King's gate,
He sought a drink for Hynd Horn's sake.

The bride came trippin' down the stair,
Wi' the scales o' red gowd in her hair;

Wi' a cup o' the red wine in her hand,
And that she gae to the auld beggar man.

Out o' the cup he drank the wine,
And into the cup he dropt the ring.

"O got ye this by sea or land?
Or got ye it of a dead man's hand?"

"I got it na by sea nor land,
But I got it, madam, of your own hand."

"O, I'll cast off my gowns o' brown,
And beg with you frae town to town.

"O, I'll cast off my gowns o' red,
And I'll beg wi' you to win my bread.

"O, I'll take the scales o' gowd frae my hair,
And I'll follow you for evermair."

She has cast awa' the brown and the red,
And she's follow'd him to beg her bread.

She has ta'en the scales o' gowd frae her hair
And she's follow'd him for evermair.

But atween the kitchen and the ha'
He has let his cloutie cloak down fa'.

And the red gowd shined over him a',
   With a hey lillelu, and a how lo lan;
And the bride frae the bridegroom was stown awa',
   And the birk and the broom blows bonnie.

An Old Ballad

ANNABEL LEE

I T WAS MANY and many a year ago,
  In a kingdom by the sea,
That a maiden there lived whom you may know
  By the name of Annabel Lee;
And this maiden she lived with no other thought
  Than to love and be loved by me.

I was a child and *she* was a child,
  In this kingdom by the sea,
But we loved with a love that was more than love—
  I and my Annabel Lee;
With a love that the winged seraphs of heaven
  Coveted her and me.

And this was the reason that, long ago,
  In this kingdom by the sea,
A wind blew out of a cloud, chilling
  My beautiful Annabel Lee;
So that her high-born kinsmen came

And bore her away from me,
To shut her up in a sepulchre
    In this kingdom by the sea.

The angels, not half so happy in heaven,
    Went envying her and me—
Yes!—that was the reason (as all men know,
    In this kingdom by the sea)
That the wind came out of the cloud by night,
    Chilling and killing my Annabel Lee.

But our love it was stronger by far than the love
    Of those who were older than we—
    Of many far wiser than we;
And neither the angels in heaven above,
    Nor the demons down under the sea,
Can ever dissever my soul from the soul
    Of the beautiful Annabel Lee.

For the moon never beams, without bringing me dreams
    Of the beautiful Annabel Lee;
And the stars never rise, but I feel the bright eyes
    Of the beautiful Annabel Lee;
And so, all the nighttide, I lie down by the side
Of my darling—my darling—my life and my bride,
    In the sepulchre there by the sea—
    In her tomb by the sounding sea.

Edgar Allan Poe

LORD RONALD

LORD RONALD was a mighty man,
A mighty man was he,
He left his lady and his land
And travelled to a far countree.

He sailed across the ocean blue
The ocean blue and bright
He sailed for many a sunny day
And many a darksome night.

He left the Lady Mirabelle.
He left her in her tower.
She watched for him and waited
Many a weary hour.

He did not come in April
He did not come in May,
She wearied of her spinning
And sighed the hours away.

She sent to him a message.
The little page returned,
"I cannot find Lord Ronald
His fortress has been burned."

She bowed her head in sorrow,
She bowed it down right low.
"Fetch me your hose and doublet,
The tidings I must know."

He fetched his hose and doublet,
She put them on with care,
She took a ship and followed
And searched out everywhere.

She searched in glen and hollow,
She searched the land around,
But not a tracing of Lord Ronald,
Her lover, could be found.

At last she heard a whisper
And followed on its trail—
The Indians have a captive
Whose cheeks are wan and pale.

She followed through the forest,
As far as far could be
Until she found the wigwams
Of a band of Cherokee.

She saw her pale-faced lover,
All bound up to a tree,
She snuck her little bodkin
And cut the captive free.

He took her for his wedded wife,
And loved her long and true;
And so shall end my pretty tale
As all tales ought to do!

An Old Ballad

LADY OF CASTLENOIRE

BRETAGNE HAD NOT HER PEER. In the province
    far or near
There were never such brown tresses, such a faultless hand:
She had youth, and she had gold, she had jewels all untold,
And many a lover bold wooed the Lady of the Land.

But she, with queenliest grace, bent low her pallid face,
And "Woo me not for Jesus' sake, fair gentlemen," she said
If they woo'd then—with a frown she would strike their pas-
    sion down:
She might have wed a crown to the ringlets on her head.

From the dizzy castle tips, hour by hour she watched the
    ships,
Like sheeted phantoms coming and going evermore,
While the twilight settled down on the sleepy seaport town,
On the gables peaked and brown, that had sheltered
    kings of yore.

And so oft she sat alone in the turret of gray stone,
And looked across the moorland, so woful, to the sea,
That there grew a village cry, how her cheek did lose its dye,
As a ship, once, sailing by, faded on the sapphire lea.

And she ever loved the sea,—God's half-uttered mystery,—
With its million lips of shells, its never ceasing roar:
And 'twas well that, when she died, they made her a grave
beside
The blue pulses of the tide, by the towers of Castlenoire.

Now, one chill November morn, many russet autumns gone,
A strange ship with folded wings lay dozing off the lea;
It had lain throughout the night with its wings of murky
white
Folded, after weary flight,—the worn nursling of the sea.

Crowds of peasants flocked the sands; there were tears and
clasping hands;
And a sailor from the ship stalked through the kirkyard gate.
Then amid the grass that crept, fading, over her who slept,
How he hid his face and wept, crying, *Late, alas! too late!*

And they called her cold. God knows . . . Underneath the
winter snows
The invisible hearts of flowers grew ripe for blossoming!
And the lives that look so cold, if their stories could be told,
Would seem cast in gentler mould, would seem full of love
and spring

                              Thomas Bailey Aldrich

LORD LOVEL

LORD LOVEL, he stood at his castle-gate,
   Combing his milk-white steed,
When up came Lady Nancy Belle,
   To wish her lover good speed.

"Where are you going, Lord Lovel?" she said,
   "Oh where are you going?" said she.
"I'm going, my Lady Nancy Belle,
   Strange countries for to see."

"When will you be back, Lord Lovel?" she said,
   "Oh when will you come back?" said she.
"In a year, or two, or three at the most,
   I'll return to my fair Nancy."

But he had not been gone a year and a day,
   Strange countries for to see,
When languishing thoughts came into his head,
   Lady Nancy Belle he would go see.

So he rode, and he rode, on his milk-white steed,
    Till he came to London town,
And there he heard St. Pancras' bells,
    And the people all mourning round.

"Oh what is the matter?" Lord Lovel he said,
    "Oh what is the matter?" said he;
"A lord's lady is dead," a woman replied,
    "And some call her Lady Nancy."

So he order'd the grave to be open'd wide,
    And the shroud he turned down,
And there he kiss'd her clay-cold lips,
    Till the tears came trickling down.

Lady Nancy she died, as it might be, today,
    Lord Lovel he died as tomorrow;
Lady Nancy she died out of pure, pure grief,
    Lord Lovel he died out of sorrow.

Lady Nancy was laid in St. Pancras' Church,
    Lord Lovel was laid in the choir;
And out of her bosom there grew a red rose,
    And out of her lover's a briar.

They grew, and they grew, to the church-steeple top,
    And then they could grow no higher;
So there they entwined in a true-lovers' knot,
    For all lovers true to admire.

An Old Ballad •

THE HOST OF THE AIR

O'DRISCOLL DROVE with a song
The wild duck and the drake
From the tall and the tufted reeds
Of the drear Hart Lake.

And he saw how the reeds grew dark
At the coming of night tide,
And dreamed of the long dim hair
Of Bridget his bride.

He heard while he sang and dreamed
A piper piping away,
And never was piping so sad,
And never was piping so gay.

And he saw young men and young girls
Who danced on a level place
And Bridget his bride among them,
With a sad and a gay face.

The dancers crowded about him,
And many a sweet thing said,
And a young man brought him red wine
And a young girl white bread.

But Bridget drew him by the sleeve,
Away from the merry bands,
To old men playing at cards
With a twinkling of ancient hands.

The bread and the wine had a doom,
For these were the host of the air;
He sat and played in a dream
Of her long dim hair.

He played with the merry old men
And thought not of evil chance,
Until one bore Bridget his bride
Away from the merry dance.

He bore her away in his arms,
The handsomest young man there,
And his neck and his breast and his arms
Were drowned in her long dim hair.

O'Driscoll scattered the cards
And out of his dream awoke:
Old men and young men and young girls
Were gone like a drifting smoke;

But he heard high up in the air
A piper piping away,
And never was piping so sad,
And never was piping so gay.

William Butler Yeats

PRINCE ROBERT

PRINCE ROBERT has wedded a gay ladye,
  He has wedded her with a ring;
Prince Robert has wedded a gay ladye,
  But he daur na bring her hame.

"Your blessing, your blessing, my mother dear,
  Your blessing now grant to me!"—
"Instead of a blessing ye sall have my curse,
  And you'll get nae blessing frae me."

She has call'd upon her waiting-maid,
  To fill her a glass of wine;
She has called upon her fause steward,
  To put rank poison in.

She has put it to her roudès lip,
  And to her roudès chin;
She has put it to her fause, fause mouth,
  But the never a drop gaed in.

He has put it to his bonny mouth,
    And to his bonny chin;
He's put it to his cherry lip,
    And sae fast the rank poison ran in.

"O ye hae poison'd your ae son, mother,
    Your ae son and your heir;
O ye hae poison'd your ae son, mother,
    And sons you'll never hae mair.

"O where will I get a little boy,
    That will win hose and shoon,
To rin sae fast to Darlinton,
    And bid Fair Eleanor come?"

Then up and spake a little boy,
    That wad win hose and shoon,
"O I'll away to Darlinton,
    And bid Fair Eleanor come."

O he has run to Darlinton,
    And tirlèd at the pin;
And wha was sae ready as Eleanor's sel'
    To let the bonny boy in?

"Your gude-mother's made ye a rare dinour,
    She's made it baith gude and fine;
Your gude-mother's made ye a gay dinour,
    And ye maun come till her and dine."

It's twenty lang miles to Sillertoun town,
    The langest that ever were gane;
But the steed it was wight and the ladye was light,
    And she cam' linkin' in.

But when she came to Sillertoun town,
    And into the Sillertoun ha',
The torches were burning, the ladies were mourning,
    And they were weeping a'.

"O where is now my wedded lord,
    And where now can he be?
O where is now my wedded lord?
    For him I canna see."—

"Your wedded lord is dead," she says,
    "And just gane to be laid in the clay;
Your wedded lord is dead," she says,
    "And just gane to be buried the day.

"Ye'se get nane o' his gowd, ye'se get nane o' his gear,
    Ye'se get nae thing frae me;
Ye'se na get an inch o' his gude broad land,
    Tho' your heart suld burst in three."

"I want nane o' his gowd, I want nane o' his gear,
    I want nae land frae thee;
But I'll hae the rings that's on his finger,
    For them he did promise to me."

"Ye'se na get the rings that's on his finger,
    Ye'se na get them frae me;
Ye'se na get the rings that's on his finger,
    An' your heart suld burst in three."

She's turn'd her back unto the wa',
    And her face unto a rock,
And there, before the mother's face,
    Her very heart it broke.

An Old Ballad

LOCHINVAR

OH, YOUNG LOCHINVAR is come out of the west,
Through all the wide Border his steed was the best;
And save his good broadsword he weapons had none,
He rode all unarmed, and he rode all alone.
So faithful in love, and so dauntless in war,
There never was knight like the young Lochinvar.

He stayed not for brake, and he stopped not for stone,
He swam the Eske River where ford there was none;
But ere he alighted at Netherby gate
The bride had consented, the gallant came late;
For a laggard in love, and a dastard in war
Was to wed the fair Ellen of brave Lochinvar.

So boldly he entered the Netherby Hall
Among bridesmen and kinsmen and brothers and all;
Then spoke the bride's father, his hand on his sword
(For the poor craven bridegroom said never a word),
"Oh, come ye in peace here, or come ye in war,
Or to dance at our bridal, young Lord Lochinvar?"

"I long woo'd your daughter, my suit you denied—
Love swells like the Solway, but ebbs like its tide—
And now am I come, with this lost love of mine,
To lead but one measure, drink one cup of wine.
There are maidens in Scotland more lovely by far,
That would gladly be bride to the young Lochinvar."

The bride kissed the goblet; the knight took it up;
He quaffed of the wine, and he threw down the cup.
She looked down to blush, and she looked up to sigh,
With a smile on her lips and a tear in her eye.
He took her soft hand ere her mother could bar,
"Now tread we a measure!" said young Lochinvar.

So stately his form, and so lovely her face,
That never a hall such a galliard did grace;
While her mother did fret, and her father did fume,
And the bridegroom stood dangling his bonnet and plume,
And the bridemaidens whispered, " 'Twere better by far
To have matched our fair cousin with young Lochinvar."

One touch to her hand, and one word in her ear,
When they reached the hall door, and the charger stood
      near;
So light to the croupe the fair lady he swung,
So light to the saddle before her he sprung!
"She is won! we are gone, over bank, bush, and scaur;
They'll have fleet steeds that follow," quoth young
      Lochinvar.

There was mounting 'mong Graemes of the Netherby clan;
Forsters, Fenwicks, and Musgraves, they rode and they ran;
There was racing and chasing, on Cannobie Lee,
But the lost bride of Netherby ne'er did they see.·
So daring in love, and so dauntless in war,
Have ye e'er heard of gallant like young Lochinvar?

Sir Walter Scott

BONNY BARBARA ALLAN

It was in and about the Martinmas time,
  When the green leaves were a-falling,
That Sir John Graeme, in the West Country,
  Fell in love with Barbara Allan.

He sent his man down through the town,
  To the place where she was dwelling:
"O haste and come to my master dear,
  Gin ye be Barbara Allan."

O hooly, hooly rose she up,
  To the place where he was lying,
And when she drew the curtain by;—
  "Young man, I think, you're dying."

"O it's I'm sick, and very, very sick,
  And 'tis a' for Barbara Allan."—
"O the better for me ye's never be,
  Tho your heart's blood were a-spilling.

"O dinna ye mind, young man," said she,
 "When ye was in the tavern a-drinking,
That ye made the healths gae round and round,
 And slighted Barbara Allan?"

He turned his face unto the wall,
 And death was with him dealing:
"Adieu, adieu, my dear friends all,
 And be kind to Barbara Allan."

She had not gane a mile but twa,
 When she heard the dead-bell ringing,
And every jow that the dead-bell gied,
 It cryed, *Woe to Barbara Allan!*

"O mother, mother, make my bed!
 O make it saft and narrow!
Since my love died for me to-day,
 I'll die for him to-morrow."

An Old Ballad

LORD ULLIN'S DAUGHTER

A CHIEFTAIN to the Highlands bound
Cries, "Boatman, do not tarry!
And I'll give thee a silver pound
To row us o'er the ferry!"

"Now, who be ye, would cross Lochgyle
This dark and stormy water?"
"O I'm the chief of Ulva's isle,
And this, Lord Ullin's daughter.

"And fast before her father's men
Three days we've fled together,
For should he find us in the glen,
My blood would stain the heather.

"His horsemen hard behind us ride—
Should they our steps discover,
Then who will cheer my bonny bride
When they have slain her lover?"

Out spoke the hardy Highland wight,
  "I'll go, my chief, I'm ready:
It is not for your silver bright,
  But for your winsome lady:—

"And by my word! the bonny bird
  In danger shall not tarry;
So though the waves are raging white,
  I'll row you o'er the ferry."

By this the storm grew loud apace,
  The water-wraith was shrieking;
And in the scowl of heaven each face
  Grew dark as they were speaking.

But still as wilder blew the wind,
  And as the night grew drearer,
Adown the glen rode armèd men,
  Their trampling sounded nearer.

"O haste thee, haste!" the lady cries,
  "Though tempest round us gather;
I'll meet the raging of the skies,
  But not an angry father!"

The boat has left a stormy land,
  A stormy sea before her—
When, O! too strong for human hand
  The tempest gather'd o'er her.

And still they row'd amidst the roar
   Of waters fast prevailing:
Lord Ullin reach'd that fatal shore—
   His wrath was changed to wailing.

For, sore dismayed, through storm and shade
   His child he did discover:—
One lovely hand she stretch'd for aid,
   And one was round her lover.

"Come back! come back!" he cried in grief,
   "Across this stormy water:
And I'll forgive your Highland chief:—
   My daughter!—O my daughter!"

'Twas vain: the loud waves lash'd the shore,
   Return or aid preventing;
The waters wild went o'er his child,
   And he was left lamenting.

Thomas Campbell

ACKNOWLEDGMENTS

Acknowledgment is made to the following publishers, authors and their books, holders of the copyright in each instance, for their permission to include the following poems in this collection:

To The Clarendon Press, Oxford, England, for these ballads from *The Oxford Book of Ballads*, edited by Sir Arthur Quiller-Couch: "The Fair Flower of Northumberland"; "The Blind Beggar's Daughter of Bednall-Green"; "The Cruel Brother"; "Lord Lovel"; "Hynd Horn"; and "Prince Robert."

To E. P. Dutton and Company, Inc., for "Colomen" from *Poems and the Spring of Joy* by Mary Webb. Copyright, 1929 by E. P. Dutton & Co., Inc. Renewal, ©1957 by Jonathan Cape.

To Julian Messner, Inc., and Isabel McLennan McMeekin, for the ballad, "Lord Donald" two verses of which appear in *Journey Cake* by Isabel McLennan McMeekin.

To Houghton Mifflin Company for the poem, "The

Warrior Maid" from *Rose of the Wind* by Anna Hempstead Branch.

To the Macmillan Company for "Host of the Air" from *Collected Poems* by William Butler Yeats. Copyright 1906 by The Macmillan Company; renewed 1934 by William Butler Yeats.

To Mr. Hugh Noyes for the poem, "The Highwayman" from *Collected Poems, Volume I,* by Alfred Noyes.

HELEN FERRIS

90157